Reflections
of
Friendship

Gentle Words in Haiku

By
Nasus & Iduji
(Susan & Judi) *Judi Hays*

PublishAmerica
Baltimore

First printing

ISBN: 1-4137-7118-1
PUBLISHED BY PUBLISHAMERICA, LLLP
www.publishamerica.com
Baltimore

Printed in the United States of America

Inspired by the Haiku of
Murasaki Shikibu as found in
The Tale of Murasaki,
by Liza Dalby

Nasus dedicates this book to:
Betty Clinard, for the gift of my first book of haiku
– July 24, 1969

Iduji dedicates this book to:
Sr. Immaculata, S.S.J., who first introduced me to
haiku
– in 1966 –
while taking a course in children's literature
at St. John College of Cleveland.

Dear Reader,

We, Susan (Nasus) and Judi (Iduji), would like to thank all our family and friends (too numerous to list) who supported and encouraged us in our dream to have our haiku published in book form. However, we do want to give special mention to Bonnie (Bonita – Atinobi) App for her time and talent, not only in her support (reading, editing, encouraging) but also in her designs and creations of greeting cards, note cards, bookmarks, etc. based on the haiku in our book.

The dream started in June of 2002, when Susan (Nasus) introduced Judi (Iduji) to a most wonderful book that she had just started to read, *The Tale of Murasaki*, by Liza Dalby. We decided to read the book at the same time, so that we could discuss it in our emails (Susan lived in Macon, Georgia and Judi lived in Ellicott City, Maryland) with one another, not knowing that doing so would start us on a year-long project.

We found that the story of Murasaki, a Japanese poet and author living in the 11th century, was not only well-written and captivating, but also poetically inspiring. Woven throughout the story were haiku poems written and sent by Murasaki and her friends, all of whom lived great distances from one another.

By the time we had finished reading the book, we both found that it had stirred within us our life-long love of haiku; inspired by the story, the two of us decided to follow the example of Muraskai and her friends and send haiku poems to one another in our emails. Despite our busy schedules, we did manage, throughout the year, to take a few moments here and there to follow our heart's desire and turn the ordinary moments of our lives into the poetry of haiku.

The following book is a collection of our haiku that reflects the everyday events of our lives from July of 2002 to July of 2003. We hope you enjoy our "contemporary" haiku, written with respect to and in the spirit of the ancient poets.

Most Respectfully,
Nasus and Iduji

A Friendship Woven
In Haiku – Thoughts and Feelings
Bringing Together

July 5, 2002

Sit beneath the boughs
Of some lovely summer tree,
With an ancient tale.

—Nasus

(Sent to Iduji along with a gift certificate
for a bookstore)

July 8, 2002

Gift of ancient tales
Read beneath the dappled shade
Of crabapple trees.

—Iduji

(Sent as a "thank you" note
for the above gift certificate)

Celebrating Life,
Years Lived and Memories Made…
The Journey Goes On

July 10, 2002

A gilded wood box
For enclosing mementos
Of the treasured past.

—Iduji.

(Sent to Nasus along with a gilded, wood
keepsake box for her birthday on July 24, 2002.)

July 17, 2002

A gilded wood box,
A memento of friendship –
Past, present, future.

—Nasus

(Sent to Iduji as a "thank you" for the gilded, wood box.)

July 17, 2002

In gilded wood box
Lay remnants of treasured past,
Tattered and faded,
Yet alive with the feel and
Fragrance of a love long past,
But not forgotten.

Nasus

(Inspired by gilded wood box)

July 24, 2002

Hot, humid, and still
The days of summer arrive.
Gifts of time and books.

—Iduji

(Purchase of "Tale of Genji" on Nasus' Birthday)

August 3, 2002

Celebrations shared –
As simple as walks and talks,
Bring glorious joy.

—Nasus

(Following a week of birthday celebrations)

August 4, 2002

Birthday memories,
Treasures to keep in one's heart,
A new year embarks.

—Iduji

(In response to above)

Words and Computers,
Friends Sending Thoughts and Feelings,
Miles Growing Shorter

July 18, 2002

At sunset – news of Nasus
Technology linking friends
No longer distant.

—Iduji

(Upon receiving email from Nasus)

August 10, 2002

Here at harbor's edge,
With a summer moon above,
Peace envelops me.

—Nasus

(In response to an email and photos from Iduji of the
Baltimore Inner Harbor)

August 11, 2002

Cheerful news and verse
Transporting friendship and love,
Solace for the soul.

—Iduji

(In gratitude for our friendship)

Years and Miles Apart,
Teacher and Student Meeting,
Spouses Leave-Taking

August 19, 2002

Raindrops fall softly,
The earth and life enduring,
Hearts weep silently.

—Iduji

(Included in letter telling of sadness after Frank
returned to Georgia where he worked)

August 23, 2002

From a chance meeting,
Like the warmth of a spring sun
Memories of youth.

—Nasus

(After meeting a former high school teacher)

August 26, 2002

Dark clouds may arrive,
Sunshine is merely hidden,
Soon to reappear.

—Iduji

(Accepting the temporary "separation" between Iduji
and Frank)

Summer is Ending,
Mind, Heart, and Soul Transforming,
Friendship Enduring

Tuesday, August 13, 2002

On my window sill
Potted ivy profusely grows,
Lifting heart at dawn.

—Nasus

("A glimpse into my kitchen at dawn")

August 30, 2002

Autumn's early chill,
Teacher sows seeds of knowledge,
Making children grow.

—Nasus

(In reference to the beginning of Iduji's new school
year)

August 31, 2002

Summer slowly fades,
Autumn previews its colors,
Learning starts anew.

—Iduji

(On the opening of the new school year)

Traveling Online,
Mind, Heart, and Soul are Soaring,
Visiting new lands

September 1, 2002

"Lightning" speed online,
Time to slowly view and browse
Places of our dreams.

—Iduji

(Planning trip and "traveling" via the internet)

September 4, 2002

Places of yore
Bring enchantment and adventure,
Life to tales we love.

—Nasus

(On viewing the websites of Yorkshire, Cornwall, and
the Cotswolds)

Gifts of Poetry
For Iduji's Grandchildren,
Composed by Nasus

A Tribute to Ariel Barouch Uy, born May 20, 2000

Definition: Child –
Breath of spring in any season,
Perfect gift from God.

—Nasus

(A poem for Ariel)

A Tribute to Isaac Barouch Uy, born September 10,
2002

Thy name is Issac.
Blest of God is thy namesake,
Blest thy father's son.

—Nasus

(On the birth of Isaac Barouch Uy – The name
Barouch means "blessed")

A Difficult Time,
Mind, Heart, and Soul Torn Apart,
Suffering and Loss

October, 2002

Clouds heavy with rain
Seem immobile in the sky,
Dark and oppressive.

—Iduji

(During a difficult time)

October, 2002

Rain droplets falling,
Heavy clouds becoming light,
Setting sorrow free.

—Iduji

(During time of sadness)

October, 2002

After nourishment,
All things refreshed and renewed.
Life abounds once more.

—Nasus

(Response to above)

Christmas Memories,
Recollections of the Past,
Joy in the Present

December 25, 2002

For quiet moments,
Treasuring life's memories,
Remembering friends.

—Iduji

(Personal inscription on Haiku book – gift to Nasus)

The New Year Enters,
Present and Future Arrives,
The Past Recedes

January 10, 2003

Friendships, like flowers
Outside a Teahouse garden,
Bloom and grow closer.

—Iduji

(New Year's Greeting to Nasus, accompanying a
Japanese card with two women in a Teahouse Garden)

Winter Ongoing,
Wind, Rain, Cold Filling the Days,
Friendship is Warming

January 11, 2003

Two months of silence,
Filled with sorrow and anguish,
A deep winter death.

—Iduji

(Reflections written in January)

January 12, 2003

Nighttime has arrived,
And the soul is still awake,
While the body sleeps.

—Iduji

(Following a restless sleep)

January 17, 2003

A gift from a friend –
A ray of sunshine
On a cloudy day.

—Nasus

(In response to Japanese card sent by Iduji)

Iduji – Nasus,
Anticipating Visit,
With insights to Share

January 17, 2003

Friendships from afar,
Visits anticipated,
Friends growing closer.

—Iduji

(In response to email)

January 18, 2003

A priceless richness,
The joy of a good friend,
The warmth of sharing.

—Nasus

(In response to email)

To Iduji: On Valentine's Day 2003

How comfortable,
How pleasant a special day
When shared with a friend.

—Nasus

(Given as a gift to Iduji following lunch on
Valentine's Day)

A Presentation,
a Day of Celebration,
Joyful Jubilation

February 28, 2003

A teller of tales,
Spinning and weaving stories,
In words and pictures.

—Iduji

(With a basket of flowers for Nasus' story
presentation at Little Carnegie of the South on 3/1/
03 and 3/2/03)

March 1, 2003

A basket of posies
Brings smile to teller of tales,
Dearest, thoughtful friend.

—Love, Nasus

(A thank you for the basket of flowers and good
wishes)

March 6, 2003

Woven brown basket
Upon my dressing table,
Sweet fragrance – friendship blossoms.

—Nasus

(Inside "Monet" thank you note for basket of flowers)

Possessed by "Romance,"
Poetry – Two Tales – Two Friends,
Possessing Oneness

Following discussions of books: *Tale of Murasaki* and
Possession

March 3, 2003

Bestowing...Sharing
Unity...Duality
Thoughts...Feelings...Friendship

—Iduji

(Email on plans for future presentation of Haiku)

March 13, 2003

Viewing stars from earth,
Receiving notes from afar,
Lifelong companions.

—Iduji

(Distance will not separate friends)

March 13, 2003

Awaiting my friend
On this early spring evening,
The man in the moon and I

—Nasus

(In response to email)

March 14, 2003

Heart and Soul flying
To be with husband - and friend
On wings in the sky.

—Iduji

(Flying down to Georgia to be with Frank and Nasus)

March 15, 2003

In Shakespeare's garden
Friends meet, words and flowers bloom,
Nectar slowly sipped.

—Iduji

(Inscription in book *Shakespeare's Garden* given to
Nasus)

March 18, 2003

Long awaited visit,
Like a breath of fresh spring air,
When had with a friend.

—Nasus

(Looking forward to visit)

Daily Ups and Downs
Bring Smiles and Laughter to Friends,
Sharing from Afar

March 18, 2003

Laughter and chatter,
Bubbles of conversations
Glimmer and glitter.

Recollections of
An afternoon of sharing,
Cheerful communion

—Iduji

(Memories of visit with Nasus)

March 18, 2003

Absent-mindedness,
Could it be old age, I fear,
With spirit so young?

—Nasus

(Included in email – with a "forgotten" question)

Springtime Arriving,
Reluctant Winter Leaving,
New Life Beginning

March 30, 2003

Tiny buds appear,
Springtime prepares her entrance,
Earth awaits beauty

—Iduji

(Spring finally showing signs of arriving)

March 30, 2003

Chilly March winds blow,
Even while cherry blossoms bloom.
Spring demands entrance.

—Nasus

(Response to Spring)

March 31, 2003

March is a trickster!
Snow arriving – covering
Spring's new flowering.

—Iduji

(Following surprise snowfall)

March 31, 2003

A lovely spring day –
My soft bed, a cup of tea,
A great tale for company.

—Nasus

(Response to "winter in spring")

April 3, 2003

At long last – teasing
Spring has crossed winter's threshold.
Farewell frozen days!

—Iduji

(Rejoicing in the sunshine and warmth)

April 5, 2003

A lovely spring day,
Warm thoughts of coming visit,
And so much to share.

—Nasus

(Anticipating visit of Iduji)

April 5, 2003

Momentary pause,
Whirlwind of errands – no time
To smell the flowers.

—Iduji

(Busy weekend with too much to do)

April 5, 2003

Worry not, my dear.
The flowers will still be there
When calm surrounds thee.

—Nasus

(In response to above email)

How Does It Happen?
Two Souls Meet by Good Fortune?
Rather, Destiny!

April 6, 2003

A friend – no, a muse,
An inspiration to me,
Nasus – my soul mate.

—Iduji

April 6, 2003

One's true self abounds,
Mutual inspiration –
Iduji, Nasus

—Nasus

Lovely Cards and Words,
Sending Flowers and Poems,
Arriving by Mail

April 1, 2003

A bowl of roses,
Like beautiful mementos,
Filled with fragrance sweet.

—Iduji

(Accompanying a Marjolein Bastin card – "bowl of
roses")

April 5, 2003

Such a special thing,
A gift in an envelope,
Fragrance of my friend.

—Nasus

(On receiving above card)

April 5, 2003

Artists splash color
Giving life to a canvas,
With paint – or with words!

—Iduji

(Accompanying Marjolein Bastin card with bowl of
flowers and paintbrush)

Springtime Holidays,
Days of Celebrating – Life
– Given for Others

April 11, 2003

Me and thee alone,
Oh dear, happy spring morning.
My heart smiles.

—Nasus

(Accompanying Easter card with spring daffodils)

April 13, 2003

Darkness enfolding
An offering of a life,
Light resurrecting.

—Iduji

(Inside Easter card to Nasus)

May 11, 2003

My friend – a mother,
Like a lovely spring bouquet,
A gift of great joy.

—With Love, Nasus 2003

(To Iduji on Mother's Day)

Traveling with Friends,
Viewing Photos, Sharing Joy,
Giving Praise to God

April 1, 2003

The thunderous falls
Spake of the earth's majesty
And its Creator.

—Nasus

(Viewing Mary Ann & Bill's photos of Niagara Falls)

June 6, 2003

Safe sojourn, my friend,
Where your spirit longs to be.
Summer solstice awaits thee.

—With Love, Nasus

(Farewell for Iduji's trip)

June 7, 2003

Come away with me
In spirit, my dearest friend,
On our adventure.

Visions of England
Will drift across the ocean
And enter your dreams.

—Iduji

(Response to farewell)

Sharing Memories
of Distant Coastlines and Moors,
a Photo Voyage

July 7, 2003

Wondrous land and sea,
Enchantment of villages,
Enticement of shores.

Entrancing Island
Calling and captivating
Spellbound travelers.

—Iduji

(Reflecting on trip to Cotswolds and Cornwall)

August 9, 2003

Transported by friends,
Land of villages, castles,
Dreams of enchantment.

Ancient times speaking
To our hearts and souls,
Through lovely sharing.

—Nasus

(To Iduji after sharing her trip to the Cotswolds and
Cornwall)

Printed in the United States
27960LVS00001BA/436-504